Collections of Reflections

Volumes 1-3:
Symphonies of Strength

Providing Inspiration through Rhythm and Rhyme

Eddie Connor

Author of
Purposefully Prepared to Persevere

AuthorHouse™
1663 Liberty Drive, Suite 200
Bloomington, IN 47403
www.authorhouse.com
Phone: 1-800-839-8640

© 2008 Eddie Connor. All rights reserved.

No part of this book may be reproduced, stored in a retrieval system, or transmitted by any means without the written permission of the author.

First published by AuthorHouse 3/20/2008

ISBN: 978-1-4343-5087-9 (sc)

Printed in the United States of America
Bloomington, Indiana

This book is printed on acid-free paper.

All scripture references are from the King James Version, New King James Version, and New International Version Bible.

Contents

Acknowledgments	vii
Dedication	viii
About the Author	ix
Preface	xii

Volume I

Power Perfected through Pain	1
The Depth of Reflection	2
No Breakdown, Breakthrough!	3
Thanks 2 U	4
The Cancer Answer	6
Thy Love	8
The Dangers of Dreaming	9
The Draped Dream	11
A Mind's Meandering Maze	12
The Cost to Floss	14
Perception vs. Reality	16
From Movement to Monument	17

Volume II

A Strange Change	21
The Stratosphere of Success	22
Musical Mansions	23
The Noose of Abuse	24
Ain't it Funny Momma?	26
Momma's Day	28
Go Bold for the Gold	30
Cancer's Cold Hard Clash	32
My Place in Space	33
Flames of Fervor, Fire, and Fortitude	34
B-Day Blessings	35
Pain and Potion	36
The Introspective College Kid	38

Volume III

Follow Your Dreams	43
The Vanished and Vanquished Vision	44
Capability: Take the Cap off Your Ability	46
The Sour Spice of Societal Ice	48
The Democratic Devastation of a Nation	49
Valuable Volition	50
The Blight of Bling-Bling	51
Alter Your Perception for Perfection	53
Liquid Lyrics	55
The Clock of Conspiracy	57
The Reclamation of a Nation	60
AMERI-coCAine	63
Afr-I-CAN Amer-I-CAN	67
2 Hard 2 Handle?	69
40-tude	72

Acknowledgments

In these following Symphonies of Strength, I would like to acknowledge my Mother, Dr. Janice Connor *(author of Propelling Faith).*

Mom, even from the days of my youth, you instilled in me the importance of educating and expressing myself. I indeed Thank You for channeling my gifts positively and challenging me to expand the parameters of my gifts, in order to enrich the world. Thank You for your love and wisdom that you continue to pour into my life.

Love,
Eddie

Dedication

This book is dedicated to young people, men, and women of all ages, races, facets, and phases in life. To the readers of my first book, <u>*Purposefully Prepared to Persevere*</u>, I trust that you have been enlightened and encouraged to elevate your life and bask in the ebullience of life.

To the child abandoned by mother or father, there still is hope to cope with the pains of life (Psalm 27:10). To the young men and women seeking to navigate the avenues of acclimation, the paths of power, the highways of healing, and the streets of success.

To the diseased, distressed, depressed, and repressed human spirit, don't give up. Keep the Faith, "You shall not die, but live and declare the works of the Lord" (Psalm 118:17).

To my family and friends, here I go unlocking my dreams again. I hope you enjoy the ride.

To my Lord and Savior, Jesus Christ. I Thank You, for your ever abounding love, gifts, and blessings that you have bestowed unto me.

About the Author

Eddie Connor, born April 7, 1982, resides in Detroit, Michigan but grew up in Kingston, Jamaica. His mother, Dr. Janice Connor (author of **Propelling Faith**) has been a missionary to Jamaica for the past twenty-one years, yet has raised Eddie and his brother Elijah to be standout men of excellence. Upon spending the early years of his life in Jamaica, Eddie affirms that his thirst for knowledge can be attributed to the British education he received in the exotic island. On his travels back to the United States, Eddie recognized the call of God on his life at the age of twelve.

Growing up in the metropolitan area of Detroit, Eddie excelled in academics, sports, and the overall structure of life. Between his Jamaican and U.S. roots Eddie could attest to the fact even at a young age, that he was different. A product of a single parent household, along with his brother, Eddie realizes that he wasn't born with a silver spoon in his mouth. Eddie was raised by a strong mother, who instilled in him life-long values and the importance of governing himself as a positive individual. These daily lessons in life prepared Eddie, for the biggest challenge of his life.

Eddie's greatest test came at the age of fifteen, on January 1, 1998, when he was diagnosed with cancer. Eddie preached his first message a few months later, after the diagnosis at the age of fifteen in Kingston, Jamaica proclaiming from Psalm 118:17, "I shall not die, but live and declare the works of the Lord." Eddie Connor affirms that he was "Destined to Overcome the Odds."

He discovered in the midst of chemotherapy treatments, radiation, nausea, hair loss, surgery, psychological, and emotional debilitating circumstances how to reach within the abyss of his soul and Resurrect Faith, Resurrect Determination, Resurrect positive thoughts, Resurrect a smile in the midst of sadness, and even Resurrect the notion of overcoming the odds.

Evangelist Eddie Connor is declaring the works of the Lord and the healing power of God has touched this young man's life, as he has miraculously been healed from cancer. Evangelist Connor is a graduate of Eastern Michigan University, having earned a Bachelor of Science in Secondary Education with a focus in History. Currently, Evangelist Connor is pursuing a Master's Endorsement, as a Reading and Literacy Specialist at Marygrove College.

Evangelist Connor is currently a teacher at University High School, in Ferndale, Michigan. Evangelist Connor influences the various sectors of academia and his surrounding community as an American Cancer Society Spokesman, Author, Educator, Evangelist, Motivational Speaker, and Radio Show Host. Evangelist Connor has garnered a plethora of awards and honors such as 2001-2002 Dean's List Award recipient; 2003 NAACP Male Student of the Year Award recipient; 2003 Kappa Delta Pi educational honor society; 2004 Martin Luther King, Jr. Humanitarian Award recipient; 2004 Eastern Michigan University President for a Day; 2004 Eastern Michigan University Ambassador; 2004 Resident Advisor Leader of the Year award recipient; 2004 Eastern Michigan University Campus Leader of the Year award recipient; and 2004 Phi Alpha Theta educational honor society member. As an author and radio show host, Evangelist

Connor shares his story of overcoming cancer in his first book, **Purposefully Prepared to Persevere.** Evangelist Connor encourages youth to overcome life's obstacles on his radio program **Youth on the March,** which broadcasts on AM 1500 WLQV, every 2nd Saturday of each month from 7 p.m. - 9 p.m., in Detroit, Michigan.

God has truly given Evangelist Eddie Connor a voice to reach individuals of all ages, races, and backgrounds in this day and time. A young man of passion, determination, and intellectual fortitude desires to impact minds in perilous times, by enhancing the lives of others and expressing the power to persevere, which will ultimately propel individuals beyond all obstacles.

Preface

Self-expression is an essential component that reveals the creative abilities within ourselves. The call for critical thinkers in a chaotic world, rings loud and clear.

Open your mind to absorb the rich vibes and rhymes of this poetic symphony. The following poems, Collections of Reflections (Volumes 1-3: Symphonies of Strength), have been cognitively crafted through cataclysmic circumstances.

In my transparency, I pray that a transformative change will transition you, from where you are to the magnanimity of where you will be.

This is your Day to Convey, This is your Season of Reason, This is your Time to Shine, This is your Hour of Power, This is your Minute to Win it, This is your Moment to Own it, This is your Year to Cheer, and celebrate the splendiferous blessings that are beckoning you to breakout and breakthrough.

In these symphonies of strength, I have placed my pain on paper, transforming it into power for this very hour.

I give you my hurts and healings, my hardships and hopes, my pains and passions, my joys and sorrows, my inspirations and devastations, my screams and dreams. I give you, <u>Collections of Reflections, Volumes 1-3: Symphonies of Strength.</u>

<u>E</u>xpect
   the
<u>E</u>xtraordinary,
       <u>E</u>ddie (E3)

Volume I

Power Perfected through Pain

Seems like yesterday,
I remember that one dark day.
Laying on my death bed,
On 1/1/98.
Thinking to myself,
Would I grow old?
Or see my dreams unfold?
The world is so cold.
Death's grip is so bold.
This ain't no common cold.
Age 15 with Cancer,
Lord give me an answer,
While these high pitched
Violins play,
Couldn't stroke my pain away.
I prayed to see the light of day,
The Lord made a way,
And I write these rhymes today.
Put my pain on paper,
Turned it into power,
For this very hour,

I saw the light in my darkest hour.

The Depth of Reflection

It's so deep,
When you look at your own life.
How far you've come,
But still how far you have to go.
I've learned,
Not to let my soul grow old,
Or grow cold,
But I gotta look to the hills,
Sky high,
'Cause my help comes from the Lord.
Death can't hold me,
Thank you Jesus,
The devil can't fold me.
Please believe this,

Your dreams are endless.

No Breakdown, Breakthrough!

I was so brokenhearted,
When Pops left at age 12,
My life restarted.
Divorce is like a family,
R.I.P,
Say goodbye,
To the dearly departed.
The pain in my last name,
Was like the chain gang,
Pulling my brain,
Divorced like Jay-Z and Dame.
Ain't no time for tears,
Restore the years,
It's time to make up,
Get ya' cake up,
Yo, you there man?
Wake up.
Dry your weeping eyes,
It's time to stand up.
This is my life,
From destitute to destined.
This is my journey,
From affliction to conviction.
This is my passion.
This is my purpose.
This is my pain.
But this is also my power,
For this very hour.

Thanks 2 U

I'm thankful for your blessings,
That alleviate my stressing,
All these times I've been depressing,
In need of your correction.
Now, I look to the hills for strengthening and protection.
Lord, order my steps in every direction.
Your love supersedes the stress and games,
To ease the day to daily pains.
Let me not be spiritually blind,
To your ever abounding love that is incomparable.
So, let today be the day of change,
Because I'm thankful to you,
Because you move and groove my life.
You're the champion of changing lives.
The Epitome of Excellence,
The Craft of Creativity,
The Endowment of Edification,
The Potentate of Power,
All I am comes from you and through you I can make it.
There's no need to fear, just dry your tears,

G-O-D will restore your years,
Because He ain't going nowhere.
In these years on earth, it seems
One can grown so old and so cold.
I used to be shy,
Now I'm more bold.
But Lord I thank you, for seeing me when I didn't see you.
For loving me, when I didn't express my love to you.
How could I have been a fool?
To turn my back on you.
Lord you saw me through and through.
You died for me,
So, I could live for you.
Thank you for redeeming my years.
Thank you for calming my fears.
Thank you for wiping my tears.
Thank you for bringing me joy, in spite of pain.
Thank you for bringing the sun out, drying my rain.
You're my claim to fame,
Oh How Great is thy name and faithfulness,
Lord increase the greatness of my faithfulness.

The Cancer Answer

I'm the Lance Armstrong of the Rap game,
I came back from Cancer,
Now the world's screaming my last name.
Any questions, just ask me
Like how could Mr. C make it back from the big "C,"
To rock the M-I-C?
It's all because of G-O-D, if you ask me.
Misty eyes,
My sky was so gray,
Diagnosed with Cancer in 1-9-9-8.
I thank the Lord, 'cause He healed me
Death's cold case couldn't kill me.
I'm still hot,
I felt the heat from Cancer's hot Glock,
Death's diseased bullets rang out, like pop, pop.
But I ain't go down like a drop top,
Poetic Pringles Pitchman, I make the top pop.

The Lord lifted me up, so I could shout Him out.
From Cairo to Crenshaw, I keep it so hot.
God provided the answer to Cancer,
It couldn't take me out.
Radiation, chemotherapy, and hair loss,
tried to make me pout,
But by Jesus stripes I'm healed,
That's without a doubt.
I've got the Victory,
If you read between the lines, you would shout out.
You can't make me doubt, what I know about.
He Subtracted my pain,
Divided my rain,
Multiplied my gain,
Added power to my last name.
The ultimate Mathematician,
Jesus is His name.

Thy Love

O thank thee for thy great love.
Thy love which heals the wounded heart,
Thy love redeems the broken heart.
Thy love which cleanses the filthy stain,
Thy love which brings the joy again.
Thy love which makes the wounded whole,
Thy love which makes one oh so bold.
Thy love binds those so torn apart,
Thy love grants one a fresh new start.
Thy love is light for the dark,
Thy love kindles the flame in one's heart.
Thy love grants grace to dream again,
Thy love breaks the shame, imbibing peace within.
Thy love grants grace and peace to mend.
Thy love grants goodwill to men.
Thy love is the compass for the sin sick soul,
Thy love provides direction for the derelict soul.
It is thy love from above that soothes the weary soul,
Providing comfort and making thee whole.

The Dangers of Dreaming

What happened to the seeds of the dreams,
Sown in the soils of our minds?
Broken down like a break dancer,
One's hope is lost without an answer,
To attain the path of privilege,
Away from the painful past of society's dark mask.
Our flags should fly at half-mast,
For the souls that lie in repose.
Yes, the millions of Africans awash in the Atlantic,
Now, we trade our fight for our fame,
To rap and rock records on Atlantic.
Performing concerts overseas,
Only to sail over the same Atlantic,
And use our fame,
To run game and perform uncharacteristic antics.
It's hope versus hardship on the hardwood,
But I'm hope's fanatic.
I know its chaotically crazy,
But don't push panic.
I'm a glutton for diamond grills,
Over destined goals.
I suppose, because commercialism declares
It's all about cash, cars, clothes,
And area codes, you know, those 304's.
But what does it profit me?
To gain the world and lose my soul.
I can't let the world, just groove my soul
And eradicate my goals.
These dreams must unfold,

But there's a danger in dreaming.
Just ask Joseph,
His own brothers jacked his coat,
And threw him in a pit to make him quit.
Just ask Jesus,
How He felt,
His homeboy Judas snitched on Him,
For some strange change,
And hung himself because of guilt and shame
The blight of bling,
Makes you rethink this thing.
When dollars don't make sense,
It subtracts the life,
You thought you've gained.
And leaves your life,
A low-down dirty shame.

The Draped Dream

Where must I begin, to mend the hearts,
Seemingly torn by greed and gain?
Capitalism's grip, has vanquished the minds of men again.
Yet, continually elevating hate.
Has Dr. King's dream become a daunting nightmare,
Without a great escape?
One must confuse and confound the haters,
Using them as elevators.
It's a chess match,
Checkmate, I'm the administrator.
I dare to not only dream,
I dare to develop the dream.
I dare to demand fruition of the dream,
I dare to be the dream.
In the face of danger,
I refuse to be a stranger.
I am the vision of my dreams.

A Mind's Meandering Maze

Mystique or Mistake,
Carefree or Caretake,
Come home don't be late.
Street lights illuminate hate.
Dark frowns can't face,
The glow and grace,
Revealed through space,
Stars twinkle without a trace.
From the atmosphere to the stratosphere,
Earth's core sheds a tear,
At the lives extinguished year by year.
Yet, one must not live in fear,
Or be controlled by fear,
Or be afraid of fear.
Fear vanquishes the vitality of one's years.
Can you witness and endure atrocities and not shed tears?

Yet, you've got an icebox,
Where your heart used to heal and feel.
Just as cold as a casket,
You hide and you mask it.
The heat of the pain,
Can melt the mind, of what your soul once felt.
Life's clashes, feel like the lashes from a belt.
Securing the sagacity of your soul
Wilt thou be made whole?
Yet, persisting questions reverberate,
In the reservoirs of your reasoning.
You ask, what's the reasoning?
It's as if life has lost its seasoning.
Oh for the day,
When you and I can hitch a ride on those healing wings.
My heart doth sing of the joy life brings,
Melody rings when faith clings,
To the hope beyond life's dreams.

The Cost to Floss

I pop the top on my drop-top,
Cruise the world.
Real deal like Holyfield,
Yo' I bruise the world.
Mission possible man,
I Tom Cruise the world.
Won't jump on ya' couch,
Like Prince, I give you diamonds and pearls.
But hold up, I gotta go platinum first.
Second thing is, I gotta let them haters disperse.
If I gave you Jimmy Choos,
Would you choose me first?
See, I gotta buy you just to make you my girl.
The game has got you name dropping,
Tags, bottles poppin'
I'm 'bout to yodel,
Like I was Mary Poppins.
Our world is oh so materialistic,
The definition of hot is oh so twisted.

Am I still blessed, if I ain't got no Bapes on?
Daddy left you and the baby girl,
Stay strong.
Sippin' on Patrón,
But your face is still long.
Got your flock of friends,
But you still feel all alone.
Got your Superman cape on,
But man you're still gone.
Really Clark Kent, inside man,
But you party on.
Got ya' stunna' shades on,
Flossin'
Like you got a hundred mill'
The thrill is so ill.
The thrill gives the world chills,
Never solves the world's ills.
So cold inside,
Frontin' outside,
Just to look hot, on the outside.

Perception vs. Reality

Cats kill for the thrill of it,
Scarface for a day,
Pacino made a mill' from it.
The streets kill over a meal for it.
The lime,
The fame,
The shine,
The bling,
Everybody wanna' floss,
Wearing rocks and rings.
Ta-dah, my claim to fame,
I made my own name,
Look Ma' I changed the game.
This world is so bold,
Even when it's hot outside,
The world is so cold.
I think I need a thin sweater,
I don't wanna' catch cold.

From Movement to Monument

Martin and Malcolm,
Sweltered in the heat of injustice.
But we got that MC Hammer attitude,
I can't touch this.
Go ahead, grab ya' hood
And ya' crew,
Civil Rights Volume 2,
We make it do what it do.
Why you turn around,
Like you looking for a leader man?
Go ahead, stand up,
Don't you know we need ya' man?
Yep, and you can even bring ya' fam'
We don't march no mo'
We ride in chrome instead.

Volume II

A Strange Change

I wanna fly around the world,
And turn it right side up.
But the world likes it where it is,
Upside down.
So, I gotta be incognito.
I'll be Clark Kent man,
I won't stroke my own ego.
My glasses sliding down
The bridge of my nose.
Came back from Cancer,
I won't lie in repose.
You reap what you sow,
Take your grills out of your mouth,
And spit some fire into your goals.
The ice made you so cold,
Bling's Blight made you so bold,
I got the cure for the common cold.
Justice or just ice?
Man is it so nice?
Can't go to weddings no more,
And just throw rice.
You gotta' throw ice.
You remixed Bob Barker,
Payed the wrong price.
Took the low road out,
Like you were Heidi Fleiss.
Pay the right price.

The Stratosphere of Success

I was waiting to exhale,
'Til I took a whiff of that
Folgers Maxwell.
My rhymes falsetto like Maxwell.
G-O-D said, "Just trust me."
I'm like Jabez,
Lord bless me.
Let my praise and worship,
Impress thee.
Touched by an Angel,
Like Della Reese.
The haters said, "No"
But God said, "Yeah, Yeah."
You're alive for a reason,
Now strive.
Don't you know,
You're gonna win that prize?
I can see the future,
Right in your eyes.
This is your day to convey,
This is your season of reason,
This is your hour of power,
This is your moment to own,
I condone it.
You've got to go through,
To grow through.
Pump the brakes,
And let God show you,
What He can do,
Through you.

Musical Mansions

Music is a passion,
Like the beat of a drum,
My rhymes boom with a passion.
These tunes are trendy, like my latest fashion
Lights, camera, action,
I give you lyrical satisfaction.
With each note I stroke,
Melodic harmonies,
Like harpsichords and symphonies.
I remedy the ills,
Bring thrills,
Constant chills.
My notes pop pills,
With endless refills of prescriptive melodies.
My rhymes don't commit melodic felonies.
It's like the music yells at me.
When music says, "Hello"
It's like Violins and Cellos,
Making sweet melodies,
My heart bellows.
I open the door to destiny.
With my Stevie Wonder,
Keys to life,
I'm rappin' in the keys of life.
An old skool'
Lionel Richie Commodore,
Infused with "My Cherie Amour."
I reply, "Hello, is it me you're looking for?"
Open ya mind,
Never shut the door.

The Noose of Abuse

Life's luster is lost,
It's about lust,
At all costs.
Broke as a joke.
You paid the cost,
To be the boss.
Rose colored glasses,
Destroy and Distract,
The masses.
Why do we continually fail,
To pass life's classes?
It's meet and greet,
Don't move ya' seat.
The world wants to introduce you,
To life's passions and fleeting fashions.
A revolving door of contraptions and attractions.
Pregnant with purpose,
You're beginning to feel contractions.
You can't numb the pain,
With novocain.

Can we call a truce?
It's no use,
Before you know it,
You're already caught,
In the noose of abuse.
Psychological pain,
Relational rain,
An Emotional game,
It's a horrible shame.
You can't be happy,
And hang,
With a noose around ya' neck.
Get control of ya' life,
Before you hit the deck.
Get off the roller coaster,
Ya' life ain't over yet.
As long as you've got breath,
You haven't seen greatness yet.
Take off the noose,
Throw off abuse,
Don't let life's problems hang you.

Ain't it Funny Momma?

Mom it's so funny,
Ya' birthday falls on Father's day.
You're not only Mother,
But a Father to me.
Single parent home,
You worked,
And educated me.
Teaching other students,
Yet, you still taught me.
About life, faith, courage,
And the simple things.
Like, how to kick a football,
That still baffles me.
She got game,
Your athletic ability, was ingrained in me.
Thanks for helping me.
I can see clearly now,
You are what,
Dad could never be.
Responsibility,
Faith,
Sincerity,

Fortitude,
Clarity,
Ambition,
Directed Destiny,
You're God's gift to me.
You show me love,
Like J.C.
Jesus Christ, if you ask me.
You've got the same intials
Like J.C.
Janice Connor, Mind-boggling.
God must have had something,
Up His sleeve.
Did He send me to you?
Or Did He send you to me?
Can't let life stress me.
I'm the first black Beatle,
I'm just go'n let it be.
I continue to see,
More of you in me.
Dr. J.C.
Thanks to you,
I'll fulfill my destiny.
You even inspire and motivate me,
To get my Doctorate degree.
You've excelled,
In raising me.
I love you Mom,
You're my blessing.

Momma's Day

Momma's Day,
Is more than just another day.
Mother's Day,
I thank you Momma, for the things you do for me.
Momma's Day,
Your love is more than a distant memory.
Mother's Day,
Ma' you mean the world to me.
Momma's Day,
You wiped the tears and sheltered me.
Mother's Day,
24-7, 365, I celebrate you endlessly.
Momma's Day,
This is your day, in addition to Father's Day.
Mother's Day,
I applaud you in May and I still laud you in June.
Momma's Day,
Like a sweet melody, you put my life in tune.
Mother's Day,
How 'bout we have a Mother's month?
Momma's Day,
Matter of fact, how about Mother's year?
Mother's Day,
Ma' your love is crystal clear.
Momma's Day,

I just wanna shed a tear.
Mother's Day,
Your love dried my tears and calmed my fears.
Momma's Day,
'Cause of your faithfulness, God restored your years.
Mother's Day,
You're the real diamond, not De Beers.
Momma's Day,
You deserve a boulevard and an avenue.
Mother's Day,
Let's go to dinner, just me and you.
Momma's Day,
Order whatever you want, off the 5 star menu.
Mother's Day,
Don't worry I'll pick up the tab too.
Momma's Day,
How ya' like that venue?
Mother's Day,
You're the delicate rose, that can never be transposed.
Momma's Day,
When I was at death's door, you spoke life and I arose.
Mother's Day,
Thank God for your love, that came my way.
Momma's Day,
Your love perfects my life, each and every single day.
Happy Momma's Day.

Go Bold for the Gold

How can you go for the gold,
When ya' soul is cold?
What profit can a man make,
If he loses his soul?
Will the day bleed light,
When ya' body's old?
Or can you go vintage,
Like a chromed out 'Olds?
Can't tell if I know,
I'm trying to open Heaven's doors,
and Hell was all I know,
'Til I heard the Savior's call.
Like a lion's roar,
Open up ya' mouth and get raw,
Not to show ya' diamond grills,
But shout ya' destined goals,

And wage war.
Take that same pain,
From the ghetto to greatness.
Turn it into power,
Yo, you know we can make this, happen.
From the suburbs to success,
Yo, the haters can't fade this.
Civil Rights Volume 2, man we can make this,
Happen again.
Take ya' house back,
So, we can take back the White House.
First you were Republican,
Than you up and thought again,
Now you're going Democrat,
Change the name to Demo-black.
Second class citizens in the USA,
Aerosmith and Run DMC, walk this way,
And go for the gold.

Cancer's Cold Hard Clash

Lying on that hospital bed,
As the doctor diagnosed me with Cancer.
My soul just froze,
My mind went cold,
My heart was broken,
Like ya' Grandma's vase,
On the kitchen floor.
I got that radiation,
But it wasn't sunlight.
I lost my hair,
And rocked the Jordan with the jersey 4-5.
My life was off-key,
And even Etta James couldn't smile for me.
I'm singing off-key,
Ooh child,
How you gonna make it out of Cancer?
My passion's for the Christ,
Now that's ya' answer.
I got one life to live, a 2nd chance Sir.
I bring that Gospel feel, like I'm ya' Pastor.
Now clap ya' hands, for ya' favorite haters,
They thought they beat ya'
But their only elevators,
To lift you to your goals.

My Place in Space

Stars and Space,
Time and Place,
Turn that Frown,
Upside down,
On your face.
Beginning and End,
Glitz and Glamour again,
Resounding Clamor,
Black holes,
and Starship probes.
Nebulous clouds,
One small step for man,
One giant leap for a space fan,
Where's my place on this earth man?
I always wanted to be,
An Astro-man.
Not the Houston Astros man.
A true, N-A-S-A man
On the N-A-S-A staff.
Houston, we have a problem man.
Single parent home,
With Mom,
But no Dad.
Oh, I felt so sad,
Now, I'm so glad.
I'm the Cancer Comeback kid,
Look what the Lord did,
Thanks Ma'
You raised a good kid.

Flames of Fervor, Fire, and Fortitude

I bring the fire,
Light Rap's Olympic flame.
You hear the beat,
Now move ya feet,
Connor is my last name.
Professor E,
College degree,
And I'm a Black man.
Yo, take a seat in my class,
You heard the bell ring.
Education, Entertainment, call it Edu-tainment.
I'm on the cutting edge,
Man, these haters can't attain it.
Going for the gold,
Ain't no platinum go'n replace it.
Running the race of life,
Yo' we're trying to make it.
Single parent home,
Momma' talking on the phone.
Wondering will that man,
Ever come home?
Baby he long gone,
Now just stand strong.
And look to God,
Because baby girl,
You can make it,
If you hold on.

B-Day Blessings

50 is the year of jubilee, plus one,
Brings the joy that Christ has begun.
A Mother of magnitude and splendor,
Mends hearts and revives souls,
From January to December.
Everyday is a day to remember,
Today is the day to celebrate your birthday.
For the world was blessed,
When a girl by the name of Janice,
Was born in June.
More melodic than a Motown melody,
Our world was in harmonic tune.
In 1953, on the 17th day of June.
From the days of Doo-Wop,
To the present days of Hip-Hop,
Dr. J. Kay will never ever stop.
As an Illustrious Educator,
Magnificent Mentor,
Benevolent Mother,
Enlightened Evangelist,
The list is endless.
You are an example of how to live,
And your love, you always give.
A symbol of freedom,
A symbol of love,
A symbol of grace,
Sent from God above.
So, Happy Birthday to you,
Because there's more in store,
Just for you.

Pain and Potion

Can you imagine,
A 15-year-old kid with Cancer?
The doctor's like hmmm,
We ain't got no answer.
Can you picture, picture
Like a deaf man with a TV,
But no caption?
Like action with no Jackson, 5
I tried to stay alive.
Wiping tears from my eyes,
Looking to the skies,
I thought I had 9 lives.
Yet, my ego disguised,
Killed the 8,
All at 1 time,
My mistake.
One life to live,
Can I dream, dream again?
If I lose, I Cruise like Tom,
On them Vanilla Skies.
If I win, I'm in,
Then I can wipe my Mother's eyes.
Lord send me a sign,

From the friendly skies.
Because these nurses are bugging
And drugging me like a dope fiend,
But man I kept my veins clean.
Because Mom was my heroine,
Like Caroline Kennedy
She broke through,
And gave me the remedy.
I've got a litany of memories.
Like that cold winter,
In Jan. of '9-8.
When my Mom,
Jan was holding my hand,
To keep the Faith.
Now, I'm making demands,
To you,
To move,
To groove,
On the path of purpose,
That God's promised to you.
It's up to you,
Your pain is Your potion,
Positioning you,
For your breakthrough.

The Introspective College Kid

Stay awake, Stay awake I say,
But no, I'm tired today.
Class is boring,
And a few people are snoring.
Yet, I can't continue ignoring,
Sleepy and tired,
Tired and sleepy.
Been up since 6 a.m.
Even my alarm clock beat me.
Get your rest,
Rest I say.
Study, study, study,
All night, all day,
Come what may,
Come with me,
What have you accomplished?
Any accomplishments today?
Anything besides,

Books, food, and friends today?
Hmm, I can't say.
Needless to say,
Will I use my time?
Or will time use me today?
When will I do what needs to be done?
How long will unhappiness rise like the sun?
If you want to make the grade,
You've got to step out of the shade,
You've got to endure the educational pains.
Flaunt your intellectuality,
Live for the truth.
Forsake the lie,
Look in the mirror,
Change your minds eyes.
Am I on God's side,
Or my side's, side?
Am I really living,
If I'm living for myself?
I gotta' eat right, workout, and
Maintain my health.
Lord help me help myself,
So, my living won't be in vain,
As I seek to provide change to life's game.

Volume III

Follow Your Dreams

Follow your dreams,
You can do anything,
If you just believe.
Follow your dreams,
You can move mountains,
Even when you just believe.
Go ahead dream again,
I believe you can achieve it when,
You believe in the Lord and yourself.
Nothing else left,
But to achieve that dream,
Make the haters and violators scream.
Baskin-Robbins,
31 flavors to my dreams.
Take the taste test,
The world's your ice cream.
Whatever you want,
You can have anything.
I got the cake and your icing,
That's the reason why I sing,
Because I fulfill my dreams.

The Vanished and Vanquished Vision

What happened to the trees,
Of the seeds of dreams sown?
Why is it people's hearts,
Are hard like stone?
Why does the world only,
Want to rock stones?
The same stones,
Are breaking young African bones.
Can we repair the single mother parent homes?
I always seemed to wonder about that 'homes.
Like why didn't the government,
Help the folks out, laying out,
Down in the Superdome?
Did that girl Katrina,
Hit by Katrina,
Did her family ever get a home?

Look at us,
We're flossin' with our diamond grills,
Never focused on our destined goals.
You know how it goes,
What profit is it to us,
If we gain the world,
And lose our souls?
Your dreams just froze.
Put some heat on your dreams,
Never grow cold,
Forever be bold.
Put on the new,
And shake off the old.
It's all up to you,
Your dreams will break you through.
Just trust and believe,
God will see you through.

Capability: Take the Cap off Your Ability

The words "I can" are mentioned,
Twice in the name Afr<u>ican</u> - Amer<u>ican.</u>
Yet, we put the letter "T" on what we can do.
We've been told we can't,
And many of us believe it's true,
Banneker, Booker, DuBois, Parks, Martin, Malcolm,
And other great men and women,
Showed us what to do.
They showed us what we can build upon and do.
Why are we acting so helpless,
Don't we know what to do?
How can we be United,
In these Divided States of America?
We're disconnected, uninformed, and misdirected.
How can we teach young men to give respect?
If no one will shield and show,
A young brotha' how to respect.
His pants are on his ankles by the way,
Yet, no one directs and guides him in the right way,
But we spectate and watch him go the wrong way.
Today's rights of passage is through the jail cells,
Not education,
No street cred' if you excel.
Ignorance is the highway,
Just stay fly and flashy.
The ladies will love you,
As long as you got ice on ya' chain,
Chrome on ya' whip,
And chirp with your Nextel.

It's so crooked and shady,
Gnarles Barkley would call it crazy.
We've become so lazy,
Our eyes are even hazy.
High off the green of greeds gain,
It's all money, power, area codes, and fame.
Buying ice grills that eventually fade,
Platinum, whips, dubs, ice, rocks, rings, and chains.
Yet, still shackled by emotional and psychological chains.
Slaves to the game,
Best consumers, worst investors.
We make someone else rich,
Then have the nerve to rock their name,
We've become so rocked by fame.
The starship enterprise of celebrity,
Is a pervading malady in society today.
The crippling manacles,
Should make us fanatical,
To fight the plight,
The blinding blight,
That darkens the vision,
Of our communal mission.
We must take back our position,
Use our intuition,
To bring about fruition,
And nourish the emotional, social, and spiritual,
Malnutrition of a nation.
We must resurrect the hearts,
Broken by devastation,
Through inspiration and motivation,
Becoming a new creation,
Eradicating a destructive destination,
For all nations.

The Sour Spice of Societal Ice

I hope these rhymes impact your mind,
In these perilous days and times.
These trying times.
The ice of injustice,
The ice of institutionalized racism,
The ice of intransigent inequality,
The ice of ignorance,
The ice of idiosyncratic negative behavior,
The ice of impassivity,
The ice of impoverishment,
The ice of indifference,
The ice is indicative,
Of a system that must be broken.
We've been trapped in a box.
Barriers and boundaries,
Have us chained and locked,
The icebox must be broken.
Its made us so cold,
But God's love,
Will defrost and warm your soul.
Our world is so bitter,
But you and I can make it better.

The Democratic Devastation of a Nation

America the Democracy?
More like Kleptocracy.
Divided states of America,
Like Erica Kane.
Look at All My Children,
Pushin' cocaine.
We kill each other with our words,
On any average day.
Able's blood cries out,
From the hands of his brother Cain.
We're stuck on ice, greed, money, fame, and gain.
American Idols,
Gangsta's are the Simon Cowell's,
Of the street game.
I'm standing on the platform,
Behind the pulpit.
Like ya' Pastor,
Tell me what's the answer?
What's the antidote?
What's the antiseptic?
For the misdirected?
This rhymes requested.

Valuable Volition

So many valuables,
So little value,
In ourselves.
Locked behind cells,
Within ourselves.
So ugly, when a lovely lady,
Sells a piece of herself.
To mend the hurt,
Down within herself.
Makes a man, kill a man,
Because he's out for self,
Lord, help that man,
Help him free himself.
You've got an ocean of problems,
They started off as a puddle.
Here's the play,
I'm the quarterback,
Just come into the huddle.
I'm down for the crown,
Yo, let's turn things around.
How 'bout you?
Will you stick around?

The Blight of Bling-Bling

Bling's blight got me so uptight,
Please believe it.
Understand you're worth more,
Than the ice on your wrist.
The shoes,
The cars,
The rocks,
The rings,
The chains,
The earrings,
The bling-bling,
The shiny things,
Sparkling.
Whether you've got Prada,
Or nada,
You've still got something,
Inside.
Even if you've got nothing,
Outside.
Don't you dare hide,
The quality,
Inside.
Over quantity,
Outside.
That gives you clarity,
Besides,
Reach for something greater than you.
Reach for your destined goals,
Not your diamond grills, dude.

We've reached for life's icy-ness,
It's time we reach for Righteousness,
Riches of righteousness.
Reach for your intelligence,
Educate yourself.
It's time out for self,
Take the Lord off the shelf.
Reach for the greatness within,
Trust me, you will win.

Alter Your Perception for Perfection

I can't afford,
To have any weak days,
During the weekdays.
I don't care what he or she say,
I need my freedom from life's trials,
Life's an Amistad,
It seems, like I'm the character Cinque.
I cultivate my character,
In the midst of life's heat waves,
Rejection is direction,
My God is my protection.
Revise your life and make corrections,
Rid yourself of meaningless indiscretions.
These are Eddie Connor's expressions,
I used to be in college and rock a program,
Called, "Exotic Expressions."
Life's a vapor full of reflections,
Yet, my mind still formulates,
A plethora of questions.
Even Einstein asked some poignant questions,
I make a point to mention,
My initials are $E=MC$ squared,
A theory of relativity,
It's still relative to me.
When you blow up,
Everyone's a relative,
Trust me.
I'm the first black Bee Gee.
Man, I'm stayin' alive,

Trust me.
A mirage at best,
Yo, that's just deception see,
I won't let the haters hinder me.
Fire shut up in my bones,
Forever its enkindling.
Ignorance alters the minds mental state,
You're committing mental felonies,
Against your mental faculties.
I'm the conductor,
Life's my symphony.
I forever compose classic,
Masterpiece melodies.
No hocus pocus,
Focus, focus,
Rhyme is my orchestral opus.

Liquid Lyrics

Reminiscent of Langston Hughes,
I compose poetic crush grooves.
Gifted with gain,
Everybody's rushing you.
Fifteen minutes of fame,
The world's got a crush on you.
Bright lights got you blushing too,
Red carpet rendezvous,
Interviews and shows,
Flying 'round,
Different area codes.
I'm a keep it cool,
You know how it goes.
The Kofi Annan Don,
Of Rap's United Nations,
Folgers coffee crystals,
My rhymes give you vivid images,
Of liquid crystals.
Uniting all races and faces,
With my lyrical persuasions,
I overcome all situations.
So noble, I go global,
I do my business in Japan,
Konichiwa, What's going on fam?
I'm Rap's official Superman.
Undercover Clark Kent,
The studio's my phone booth man.
Cancer couldn't kill me,
Because the Lord had a plan.

Again and again, I rejoice,
With organs blaring,
In my Sunday Preacha' voice.
Rap music's Apostle,
Presiding Bishop of Gospel.
Coming to America,
I let my Soul Glow like Arsenio.
Good morning America,
Like Erica Kane.
As The World Turns,
My game remains the same.
I'm numb,
Because fame's my novocain.
The world is high,
Off celebrity cocaine.
Publicly successful,
Privately dreadful.
All my rhymes are credible,
Eat my words they're edible.
A buffet of belief,
I provide nutritional relief.
Absorb the positive,
It's plentiful.
Why do we choose,
To choose what's pitiful?

The Clock of Conspiracy

2 index fingers in the air,
Forms the letter "V."
Fixin' to be out like Nixon,
Peace.
Hip-hop in,
Let the neighbors,
Watch the chrome spin,
On my '83 cherry candy painted Bonneville.
It's a time machine, if you will.
Back to the Future,
I'm so fly,
You can call me, "Marty Mc Fly."
Dr. Emmett Brown makes me,
Think of a brown boy named,
Emmett Till.
The thought of him,
Gives you brain freeze,
Like ice cream,
A cold chill.
His murder was ruthless, so ill.
No Advil can soothe the pain,
I feel.
Zoom back in time,
In my cherry candy painted Bonneville,
Rewind the time, 20 times.
Maybe we can change the times.
And rearrange the world,
This time,
Before it's too late,

Man, we're too late.
11/22/'63,
JFK in Dallas, Texas,
Faced the day of perpetrated malice,
On that grassy knoll.
4/4/'68,
Shots rang out with hate.
MLK dropped down,
On that top balcony floor,
Of the Lorraine Motel,
A crying shame,
Did Coretta scream or even yell?
6/5/'68,
RFK's brains emptied out,
On a hotel kitchen floor.
Bullets blasted,
From a .22 caliber,
By a 24-year-old,
With a lack of caliber.
JFK, MLK, and RFK,
Who was the mastermind behind those dismal days?
Could it have really been the KKK or LBJ,
Mafia, foul play, or did J.Edgar Hoover have his way?
Forever, I see Medgar Evers,
A few steps from home,
Right outside his home.

Popped by haters bullets in his back,
Justice didn't step up,
It took a step back.
The haters never confront,
Or come front,
But always stab you in the back.
A few steps from greatness,
The enemies want to pull us 2 steps back.
No time to slack,
I must succeed.
Please believe it,
That's a fact.
The light doth shine bright,
Yet, darkness seeks to take its toll,
On our life.
All striving to gleam from the green,
We seem to get caught up,
In the black and white color schemes.
It's all a conspiracy,
Don't you see?

The Reclamation of a Nation

How can we reclaim a nation,
That is bound by the manacles,
Of capitalism, perversion,
Frustration, and degradation?
In the words of Langston Hughes,
Let America be America again,
But I propose to you,
Where does America begin?
From the ghettos and gangs,
To our brothers locked behind,
Physical and psychological chains.
From teenage pregnancies,
To economic difficulties.
From drive-bys,
And chalked out crime scenes,
To sexually explicit music videos,
And violence on the TV screens.
Have we become more technologically minded,
Yet, day-by-day morally slighted?
How can we reclaim a nation,
When our hopes and dreams,
Are nestled in the hearts of young people,
Who are often confused,
Because they've been misused and abused?
Fathers have fallen and Mothers are crawling,
To pick up the pieces that have been left behind.
Politicians are speaking,
And Preachers are preaching,
But is anyone reaching,

Out to the lost,
So they can be found at any cost?
Where have the leaders gone,
That seek to uplift our society?
What happened to the sound of feet,
Marching for justice?
Where is the strength that will,
Hew out of the mountain of despair, a stone of hope?
Where is the love, that will embrace the hater?
Where can America turn,
When it has turned on herself, and her creator?
Yet, in order for America to be,
It must begin inside of you and me.
In order for America to be,
Christ must live in our hearts,
Where He can invigorate spiritual liberty.
So, for all who read this decree,
Let not your heart be troubled.
For the answer to the reclamation of a nation,
Is found at the Cross of reconciliation,
That will wipe away the tears,
Of frustration and degradation.
So, for this to become true,
It must begin inside of me and you.
Not just in the White House,
But your house.
Not just on the westside.
But your side.
For the band of brotherhood,
And the serenity of sisterhood,
Must begin in your neighborhood.
In order to breakdown the walls,

That blockade our benevolence.
Yet, in order to rehabilitate,
The debilitated state of our nation,
We must be determined,
Dedicated, and devoted, to uplifting humanity.
Yet, remain connected to the divine power of Christ.
For this cannot be all of me and none of thee.
For the Declaration of this great nation,
Was built upon togetherness, freedom, and equality.

AMERI-coCAine

The world is so crazy,
I gotta keep my soul clean.
I'm like Spike Lee,
Man, you know I <u>Do The Right Thing</u>.
What if teachers were celebrities?
Think about it,
They taught and teach celebrities.
Stand in line,
Come and wait,
Meet Mr. and Mrs./Ms. so and so,
Won't that be great?
Don't take advantage,
Their paychecks show,
There's no advantage, given to them,
It's outlandish, what we're witnessing.
90 million to throw a ball through space,
Inaccurately.
90 dollars to throw the ball of education,
Accurately,
And that's all.
Just to sub on an average day,
For an 8 hour day,
In order to shield children,
From going to jail cells,
Yet, one must quiet the quells,
Of disrespectful yells.
Tell Samantha and Sean to wake up,
For their work, they must make up.
While shaking your head, you wonder why,

The guy behind the sleeping guy,
Uses the foil for the gum wrapper,
To make a diamond grill,
And smile endlessly at will,
Showing off his bling foiled grill.
While a girl beside him continues to sing,
"Smile for me Daddy, I wanna see your grill."
Watch the educational tight rope,
Don't let the drink of destiny spill.
I continue to feel the cold,
As the loss of consciousness chills my soul.
How will these children be when they grow old?
Not all classrooms are this way,
Yet, some classrooms are this way.
Please pray for the hired teacher,
Coming back the next day.
I gotta get out of this teaching game,
We ain't getting paid nothing.
In this academic hustle,
You gotta' have a side hustle.
Legal of course,
I can't get off course.
I'm trying to hit a hole-in-one,
On this educational golf course.
Teaching is,
The most important job,
With the least provisions.
Do we have an educational vision?
America wake up, the system needs a revision.
We've lost the grips on our mission,
Poor kids can't get a rich education.
No child left behind,

Running the nation.
Leave the kid behind,
Affect the money you're making,
Got us living like paupers,
With the pennies we're taking.
I'm putting the government on blast,
At last,
Take the money,
Dump it into education.
Flip the frowned face,
Of the youth in our nation.
We're manning the Iraqi stations,
Flooded with youth,
Dying for a lie,
Rather than the truth,
More money, ice, greed, and gain.
Oh my, gotta love temptation,
Eradicating the youth of our nation.
Take the money from the oil,
And place it on the squeaky minds,
Of the uneducated kids in urban communities.
We're dumping money into jail cells,
By dumping kids into educational and societal hell.
Scratch the surface of sagacity,
Like DJ Grandmaster Flash,
Scratchin' the needle on a record.
Raise the bar and watch it get better.
Raise the destitute to destined.
Resurrect and redirect.
Review, revise, and revive.
Regenerate and restore.
I implore,

Let us not revolve,
Through the destitute door.
Refute that which is of ill repute,
We can no longer ignore society's scream,
And hit "mute" on a kid's dream.
Chalk it up into a crystallized dream,
No pain, no gain.
Is it really ours or societies shame?
Where are the medicinal pills,
For societies ills?
Can we ever erase the pain,
In the land of AMERI-coCAine?

Afr-I-CAN Amer-I-CAN

I can vs. I can't,
I will but I'll wait,
On time vs. too late,
Take the "T"
Off the word "Can't."
I'm labeled as a person,
Who can,
Twice more than,
I even think I can.
So nice,
Please believe,
You can twice man.
Afr-I-CAN Amer-I-CAN,
I know I can,
Because success is in,
My mind and hands.
Pat yourself on the back,
Even if no one else has.
Stay on the purpose path,
Motivate yourself,
To pass life's class.
Unity will birth,
The real U and I,
In society,
To eradicate impropriety.
Let's build a foundation of love,
Light the cauldron of legacy.
I can do more with less,
Because I was born to be the best.

You can keep the scraps,
I refuse to settle for the rest,
My mind is on a mission for the best.
I CAN forgive the hater and perpetrator.
I CAN use the key of education,
To unlock the doors of elevation.
I CAN be bold and stand for right, in the face of wrong.
I CAN refuse to call my brothers and sisters, "Niggas,"
No longer assassinating their self-confidence,
No longer pulling the self-hatred verbal triggas.
When will we decide enough is enough?
And that I will no longer shoot down,
My brothers or sisters,
Self-esteem and deter their dreams.
Afr-I-CAN = No limits to my dreams.
Amer-I-CAN = I will pursue my dreams.
Afr-I-CAN = No limits to my life.
Amer-I-CAN = Today I will live my best life.
Afr-I-CAN = No limits on my mind.
Amer-I-CAN = I will cultivate the intellect of my mind.
Afr-I-CAN = No stressing.
Amer-I-CAN = I've been provided the blessing.
I CAN
I CAN
I CAN
I CAN
I CAN do all things through Christ, which
Strengtheneth me, (Philippians 4:13).

2 Hard 2 Handle?

So, you think you have it hard, huh?
We talk about this and that is too hard.
I can't do this,
I can't do that,
I'm too tired,
I'm giving up.
Well, check this out,
I'll tell you what's hard.
What's hard, is being diagnosed with,
Cancer as a young teen.
What's hard, is receiving chemotherapy,
And radiation, daily.
What's hard, is after the chemotherapy and radiation,
You walk into the next room,
And feel the surge of a syringe,
Sliding through your spine,
To extract spinal fluid.
What's hard, is after the spinal tap,
You lay backwards,
For three hours, in order to regulate your body.
What's hard, is calling for a bucket, before you vomit.
Because you feel yourself getting nauseous,
Just as sick as a dog.
What's hard, is waking up the next,
morning to an alarm clock,
Only to find,
That your white pillow sheet is covered,
With the follicles of your hair,
That fell out while you were sleeping.

What's hard, is realizing that the barber didn't,
Cut your hair while you were sleeping.
What's hard, is realizing that the poison,
Of chemotherapy and radiation,
Was the Delilah that cut all your hair off.
What's hard, is rising up out of the bed, in utter amazement.
What's hard, is walking to the bathroom mirror and running,
Your fingers through your hair,
Only to watch the follicles of your hair,
Cover your hands and fingers.
What's hard, is screaming to the top of your lungs,
Dropping tears, because you realize,
Your body is disintegrating before your very eyes.
What's hard, is your mother running to that same bathroom,
To hold and comfort you, through the HARD times.
What's hard, is eating the distasteful beets,
Mom cooked, in order to keep my blood levels high.
What's hard, is trying to spit the beets out,
Or place them in a napkin,
When Mom isn't looking and toss them in the trash.
What's hard, is always getting caught by Mom,
And in return for my efforts,
More beets are placed on my plate, by a loving Mom.
What's hard, is having the absence of a Father,
To further you along, on the fateful road of Cancer.
What's hard, is coming to grips,
With the fact that your Mother is mentally stronger,
Than your recalcitrant Father,
Who doesn't understand,
What it means to assume responsibility,
For his Cancer fighting son.
What's hard, is going to a church,

Where everybody remembers you one way,
Yet, a few months later,
You walk in another way,
With a bald head and 60 pounds bigger.
What's hard, is walking up the church aisle,
With folks looking at you,
As if you have the modern day form of leprosy.
What's hard, is watching those same individuals,
Whisper to each other about your appearance.
What's hard, is realizing those same whisperers,
Were your friends, just a few months ago.
What's hard, is after being healed from Cancer,
You come across an old acquaintance,
In a shopping store,
You say, "What's up?"
Rather than a reply with "Hey, Hello, or What's up?"
All they can articulate is, "I thought you were dead."
What's hard, is holding your right arm back,
Releasing your balled up fist,
And using every fiber of self-restraint within you,
Because you want to knock them into next week.
What's hard, is typing these very words to you,
Recalling the memories of the pain, shame,
And psychological chains.
What's easy, is drying the tears,
Informing you that your situation(s) will get better.
What's easy, is understanding the experiential knowledge,
Of what it's like to struggle through hard times,
And live through dying situations.
What's easy, is allowing God,
To regenerate and reinvigorate my life.
Now you tell me,
Is your life really, 2 HARD 2 handle?

40-tude

Dr. Martin Luther King, Jr. never saw 4-0
The tragic hands of time,
Stole his time,
Close to 40 years ago.
Was it a Smith & Wesson,
.40 pistol that caused the pain?
America divorced the truth,
And kept the .40 karat wedding ring.
Alienated with no alimony,
Where's my 40 acres and a mule homey?
The King's legacy remains,
Yet we're still locked,
Behind psychological doors and chains.
The greatest American who never reached 40,
Age 39, the end of his time,
But not his story.
And they say life begins at age 40.
I gave you 39 poetic rhymes and reasons,
To wake up out of your 40 winks of sleep.
Turn off the snooze button of your life.
It's time to run, run, run,
No time to creep,
O Mary don't you weep, weep, weep,
Mount up on your feet.
Isaiah 40:31,
Go with God, you're number 1.
I know it's been dark,
But here comes the sun.
Because of the One,

Who gave his Son.
Brush your shoulders off,
They can't touch you son.
Haters are your elevators,
Life's the 40-yard dash.
Sprint and score a touchdown,
Here's your chance,
Do your dance.
Take advantage of life's chance,
It's your world,
You can bring about change,
Yet our world has profoundly changed.
Blinded by the lights, cameras, and action,
We fail to take positive action.
Societal shackles,
Psychological chains,
You do yourself an injustice,
Thinking your value resides in,
Bling, rocks, and rings,
Fame, chains, and things.
Partyin' in clubs 4-0, 4-0,
On the stage of life,
You forego the show.
40/40,
Crystal clear,
Diamonds sparkle crystal clear.
When you go'n stop,
Sippin' Cristal dear?
Your daughter, Crystal,
Needs you to wipe her tears,
Calm her fears,
In her child, teenage, and young adult years.

Rub your eyes,
Is your 20/20 vision clear?
Momma's working 40 plus hours a week,
Wondering, will her kid,
Use her education,
So she can fly in first class seats?
No father in the home,
Age 14, looking grown.
Young fellas and 40-year-old men,
Trying to take her home.
She's blinded by the whip,
Sitting on 24-inch chrome.
He's sippin' on a 40, smoking hydro'
Sparkles in her eyes,
When she glances at the 40 diamonds,
In his chain alone.
Inside she's all alone.
A potential father figure, to her,
Numerical digits and measurements,
He's trying to figure out first.
Spittin' game for 40 minutes,
She thinks he wants to know her.
He knows it's a game,
Only in it to win it,
No shame in his game.
Any minute now,
She could trod the path of pleasure,
When it takes years to erase the pain.
39 poetic rhymes
yours truly, Eddie Connor,
My ambition is to change the game.
Number 40,

Don't get left behind,
Put that on everything.
40 the concluding poem,
Yes, Symphonies of Strength.
The 3 volume series,
Composed and orchestrated.
It's your future,
You create it.
The number 40,
Making history.
Graduated from college,
I majored in History.
Wonder will today's kids,
Ever appreciate their history?
Possibly a mystery,
Don't miss the story.
39 poems ago,
I gave you my story.
If 40's the new 20,
At 25,
Where does that put me?
Never thought I'd see 16,
Much less 40.
Age 25, less than half-way to 40.
Martin was the Moses,
I'm this generation's Joshua man.
40 years passed on,
Still no plan.
I'm taking you,
Out of the wilderness,
Into the promised land.
40 days and 40 nights,

Rainy situations,
Flooded ya life.
But you made it,
Out alright.
You're the Noah,
Of your New Orleans,
Overcoming your chaotic Katrina,
Through God's ark of blessings.
40 is the number of grace.
In this 40th poem,
Reclaim your space.
I charge you,
To take back your place.
Tell the devil get back,
Tell the haters,
This is Myspace,
Dot-com,
The battle is the Lord's,
And I have overcome.
Yes,
I can remain calm.
Forget the past,
Forge past your past.
Fortify your mind.
Like the 1849er miners,
discover your gifts and talents,
Be your own gold miners.
Don't let 40 years go past,
Throw off the bowlines,
Sail past your past.
40 months,
40 weeks,

40 days,
40 hours,
40 minutes,
40 seconds flew right past you.
Don't let your dreams sail past you.
What will you do?
I ask you.
40 is the number of renewal,
Be renewed.
40 is the number of revival,
Be revived.
40 is the number of grace,
Receive it.
40 is the number of dominion,
Walk in it.
Without further ado,
This is my ode to you.
Use this poetic 40-tude,
To introduce you,
To the NEW YOU!!

Contact Information:

To invite Eddie Connor to speak at your church, conference, event, or school, please write to the following mailing address or email:

Mailing Address:
Eddie Connor
29488 Woodward Avenue, Suite 215
Royal Oak, Michigan 48073

Email:
EConnorjr@aol.com